Made with ❤ on the BookLeaf Publishing Platform

www.bookleafpub.in

www.bookleafpub.com

Romance, Rants & Revolutionary Thoughts

Because poetry is cheaper than therapy!

Disha

BookLeaf Publishing

India | USA | UK

Dedication

To those who press play on soul-warming songs, just
before returning to their bartered lives —
I see you.

Preface

This book was born in the quiet chaos of late-night thoughts and early-morning heartbreaks. It is a collection of everything I felt deeply, spoke too loudly, or buried too silently. It's for the lovers who've burned in their passion, the rebels who raged in their silence, and the everyday revolutionaries who dare to feel in a world that demands numbness.

Romance, Rants & Revolutionary thoughts isn't a genre, it's a state of being. It is what happens when your soul refuses to choose between tenderness and fire. Here, poetry is tangled in protest, prose dipped in nostalgia, and rants on the back of old love letters. These are pieces of me — raw, wounded, laughing, healing. Some are celestial, some melancholic, some loud like a war cry, and others soft like a memory you only revisit when no one's watching.

This book doesn't promise answers. But it offers a mirror. A moment. A heartbeat. Welcome to the chaos. Welcome to the calm. This is for you. In here, you will find romance, rants, and revolution in love, womanhood, and life! For the ones who dream with their eyes open, love without logic, question the rules, and still choose to stay in all their broken, beautiful humanness.

— Disha

Acknowledgements

To the people who stayed through my silences, breakdowns, monologues, and mood swings.Thank you for holding space for my chaos. To every soul who unknowingly became a character, a metaphor, or a moment in this book.Thank you for existing the way you do. You left marks that turned into meaning.
To my quiet supporters, the friends who read my work before it was "work," who listened to my wildest ideas like they were gospel, and those who never flinched at my intensity, you made me feel heard before the world did. To the poets, rebels, lovers, and thinkers who came before me, whose words made me feel less alone in mine. To the nights that broke me and the mornings that built me. Thank you for teaching me that resilience and softness can co-exist. May you find something here that reminds you of yourself. The parts you celebrate, the parts you hide, and the parts you've just begun to understand. And lastly, to Time. For being cruel, kind, endless, and intimate. This book would be nothing without your strange poetry.

With all my messy love,

-Disha

1. "Of Forts, Revolution and Love"

I've been to forts,
palaces, and dreamlands,
the remains of insipid yellow houses,
drenched in the pain of longing.
The infinite restlessness,
soaked in the half-buried bodies.
unreceived, unread love letters
in the backyards of broken houses.
ancient laced pale pillow covers,
Bathed in the tears of revolution.
embellished greenish-grey curtains,
hiding the bodies of miserable women.
I saw romantic men,
dying revolutionaries.
I saw revolutionary women,
dying romantics.
I saw screaming, shouting walls
dying ranting about life.
I saw Revolution loosing to Love.

2. "A Revolution Left Behind"

I lay there on a sweaty afternoon, on the coldest bed.
with my brain detecting a fly,
I couldn't remove it from my face!
I recollect wearing a pair of brown-looking black boots.
For sure, I cannot feel it.
Where is my peachy hat?
Jonathan adored it.
My grey waistcoat was drenched in blood.
Oh, the nightmare!
My wedding ring? For God's sake!
Jonathan brought that green diamond from Iraq!
For the first time in fifty years, I can not feel it!
My uncombed long lusty hair, are spread like branches
of,
that ancient banyan tree outside our neighbor's gate.
Why is my watch not ticking?
Why are my nails not done?
Is the oven ready?
I'm trying to detect the smell of that freshly baked cake.

Jonathan, can you get that for me?
Where is my seventh sense?
Jonathan? Jonathan?
Are you even listening?
Am I just a dead old woman to you now?
Did I die of love?
Where is my share of rebellion?
After all these years of romance,
Are you offering death,
As a revolution to me?
Jonathan, answer me! Peel back the silence,
open my eyes, if you dare.
Is this what love becomes—
a quiet burial, a whisper in the dust?
Did I not love loud enough?
Did I not scream revolution?
Between our sheets, between our breaths?
I know you will move on,
Live or die in your favorite ways.
But, my love!
The revolution of my warm kisses,
the rebellion of my cuddles,
the mutiny of my fingures on your bare chest,
will echo in the walls of your heart!
Jonathan, do you hear me now?

3. "Where Rivers Burn!"

I was always at odds with love.
Never found peace in the arms of a stranger.

Love made me weak and vulnerable.
A never-ending red signal on roads I was meant to race.

Life was the river, and love was the friction.
Dragging my current, slowing my storm.

But I craved it like a moth to the flame.
Like revolution to silence, dangerous, yet divine.

Love asked me to soften, I offered fire instead.
They wanted surrender, I gave Storms instead.

Because how do you hold hands
when yours are busy breaking chains?

4. "The Revolution Beneath My Skin"

I watched it happen–
Those pigments turn into a tide.
The wave wasn't blue.
It was every unsaid thing
I swallowed to stay afloat.
It looked like that powerful dream
that never let me sleep
when I was six.
It felt like the death of a star
or the birth of a nucleus.
Sagittarius B, with its event horizon,
expanding around its center of gravity.
I assumed I was falling sick—
or getting well,
once and for all.
I caught my breath and
gathered courage to witness
that once-in-a-lifetime moment.

And in that stillness,
time stumbled
like even it forgot how to move
without pausing
to witness something sacred unfold.
The moment I saw his eyes
the eyes of a man falling in love.
His gaze, once still as winter lakes,
now shimmered with the tremble of spring.
A soft unfurling of light,
as though dawn remembered
how to blush.
They lingered—
not just seeing form
but the revolution beneath my skin.
The poetry in a glance.
Each blink—
a breathless stanza
written for me and me alone.

5. "The Woman the sky couldn't Hold"

She draped the ocean in the pleats of her maroon saree,
freeing the edges like unbridled waves.

She adjusted her black bindi—
the moon among stars in an infinite sky.

Rose-petal extracts stained her cheeks,
echoing the tender hues of a setting sun.

Her lips, the shaded red horizon—
where the sky and sea meet in reverence.

She wore the gravity of the planet
in the glint of her tiny earrings.

Her hair danced wildly
like sea winds at the shore of an unnamed island.

Her neck was the bridge,
between two war torn, disconnected, dangling countires.

She walked like a scenic sunset, gathered and admired
with the same breathless wonder, day after day.

Her smile: memorable, mysterious,
like nature's deepest unsolved secrets.

Her footsteps hummed with forgotten lullabies—
songs sung to children of displaced lands.

Her silence spoke in dialects of longing,
of roots pulled, of wings grown from ache.

Even the constellations paused—
recharting maps by the light of her becoming.

And she shone like,
a North Star in the night sky,
divine, and crystal clear.

6. "Subconscious Sedition"

She was like poetry—
dark and aesthetic,
burned and patched,
stitched together by scars and stars.

She carried an aura—
the magnetic pull of Earth,
the quiet gravity of elegance.

A homeless mess,
yet always
a story on her lips.
Something to say.
Something worth hearing.

She collapsed against your skin,
and her spirit wove itself
into your fable—
a chapter
in your unfinished book.

She was sharp.
She was curious.
No clear beginning,
no clean end.
Just presence—
chaotic, consuming,
and beautifully undefined.

You loved the uncertainty.
The unpredictability.

She made you a part of her—
quietly,
completely—
by claiming the most vital part of you:

She had your subconscious.
And because of that—
she had you.

7. "The Glow Of Hope"

I want women to feel the deepest scar beneath their
belly,
a mark of motherhood—
or a wound from the battlefield.
To stand tall, radiant,
with the glow of hope.
To unravel their miseries
with vivid luminosity,
enlightening rooms
with the brilliance of their being.
Let their saree-drapes carry
the diversity they so boldly embrace.
I want women to rise like
corals in cyclones,
be shelter in rainforests,
and stand as firm as the Himalayas
against the western winds of change.
With strength to balance life and death in each breath,
blending traditional remedies with artificial intelligence.

Women must rise like the Great Wall of China
against societal adversity,
confront misunderstood modernity
with rooted grace.
Let them stand
at the forefront of *Atma Nirbhar Bharat*,
grabbing small-scale dreams,
commanding diplomatic pivots.
I want women to face
their fiercest fears,
to master the unknown,
to understand their tears.
To break free
from unauthentic traditions,
discard futile emotions, and embrace awareness
of policies, of rights, of power long withheld.
I want women to claim their sensitivity as strength,
to feel every touch, and demand equality.
I want women to simply be women.
Unapologetically.
Completely.
Magnificently.

8. "Mangroves before the Sea"

I've seen women,
Stronger than Tsunami waves,
Softer than volcanic ashes.

They had hearts of gold,
Hands of steel,
and a smile worth of million suns.

They were fantasized by men,
For their indian curves,
And the beauty of the Greek goddess.

Their faces lit like thousands of fireflies,
Sweeter than honey,
Calmer than sunflowers.

They cried a little too easy,
and cared a little too much
even about the things they never shared.

They stayed silent when impatient,
they stood like mangroves before the sea,
for the things they found right.

They were the muses in every painting,
They were both loved and hated
they were revered, and still betrayed.

They walked through
storms in stilettos,
and stitched their scars with poetry.

They nurtured broken homes
and blooming dreams
in the same breath without faltering.

And when the world forgot their worth,
They rewrote their
Stories in fire.

They wore sarees spun in silk,
Sometimes kurtas of pashmina,
But Self-respect?
It was their favourite accessory.

9. "Metamorphosis is a Revolution"

The fatal death of caterpiller,
made the butterflies ponder.
The eventuality of life and
the cost of survival.
They were infuriated at the flowers,
for their beauty had lured it in.
for the soft petals had whispered promises
of nectar-laced dreams.
For the winds had sung lullabies
that carried the caterpillar toward its fate.
The alluring, warbling creature
had danced around them,
its mere presence a revolution,
turning the garden into a canvas
of movement, color, and change.
But beauty, it seemed, was not meant to last.
Days later, it lay shriveled,
a forgotten body on the soil,
undefined and formless,

a life cut short before its wings
could even touch the sky.
The butterflies, trembling with rage,
looked toward the gardener—
the wielder of shears,
the master of order,
the dictator who lived
and who perished.
He never understood the *metamorphosis.*
To him, insects were mere involuntary creatures,
accidental lives in his perfect world.
He killed with indifference,
with a flick of his wrist,
with the certainty of one
who had never known what it meant
to transform and survive.
And yet, the butterflies knew.
They had been caterpillars once.
they had crawled through the dirt,
borne the weight of fragile skins,
split open under the burden of becoming.
and for that, they mourned.
and for that, they raged.
For they knew, in a world like this,
TRANSFORMATION was the most dangerous thing of
all.

10. "Mocked by the Stars"

It's another cloudless night—
stars hang like soft-lit streetlamps,
and sleep has left
without saying goodbye.
The sky is loud and clear
with its quiet message
of what lies beyond.
As if it wants to tell me:
You are a part of *INFINITY*

But it also mocks me—
with the union of life and death,
with the fragility of my breath,
My quiet merging with *SINGULARITY*

11. "How Do I Want To Die?"

With faith in my heart
and a smile on my face.
With grace in accepting
my futility.

With the warmth of lives I've touched and
the belief that I laughed and cried enough.
With a heart healed—
though broken many times.

With the quiet confidence
that I always tried.
With love and passion
filling my soul.

With the strength of knowing,
I worked toward a goal.
With the courage to stand for what's right
and the awareness of my mind's true might.

With contentment
that I never turned away,
and the hope
I'll be remembered the right way.

With tears that watered
the seeds of my growth
and laughter that
echoed in empty halls.

With stories etched
in the corners of my soul,
and dreams I dared to chase
even when small.

With a will to live more—
yet no regret,
and the knowledge
that whatever time I had was enough.

12. "Melody in the Mahyem"

So stuck,
ringing a rhythm to this life,
or if it ain't rhythm,
a music to this nuisance.
Taught to live for a dream
but never learned how to **target a day.**
What did you teach me, Miss Lal?
How to survive the late twenties
was never on my school syllabus!
Busy acing debate competitions,
never noticed the trophies—
They rust, too.
Finding melody in life's oscillations—
so hard.
So hard, Miss Clifford!
How to stay busy constructive,
without letting my brain know I'm trying—
No one warned me.
The Class on "Evolution of Geographical Thoughts"?
Sorry, Shabbir Sir—

It's not evolving my emotional topography.
Tell me:
what to like,
what to hate,
whom to vote for,
what to taste.
Maybe a routine?
Just one?
The school syllabus needs a revolution—
less algebra, more answers like:
how to accept,
how to move on,
how to make peace with defeat.
How to unclench the jaw
when the world won't soften.
How to build a home in chaos
without mistaking pain for permanence.
How to stay tender and still not break.
How to hear the melody
in the randomness of destiny.
How to take a daily walk
with this miracle called—
LIFE!

13. "Eat the Fog"

Hug the one you want to.
Not the one you're supposed to,
not the one they say fits your story.
But the one who makes you feel like sunlight
spilled on skin after a long storm.

Spill that biggest secret—
the one eating away at the corners of your ribs.
Say it out loud,
even if your voice cracks like old vinyl.

Liberation sometimes sounds like shivers.
Eat your favorite food—
with your hands, with abandon.
Don't count the calories.
Count the sighs of relief
as it touches your soul before your stomach.

Be known.
Not for perfection,

but for drama,
for wit,
for your fancies and your ridiculous theories on love,
for the way you romanticize dusty libraries
and make poetry out of panic attacks.

Find a home in the wilds.
A shack made of quiet moments.
A hut built on howling freedom.

Run barefoot into winter.
Let your toes numb,
your soul ignite.
Let the cold remind you:
You're still alive.

Feel the mist on your face.
Let it sit there like a secret.
Eat the fog.
Devour mystery,
bite into the unknown.

Reside in woods.
Talk to trees.
Let leaves name your loneliness.
Send obnoxious texts.
Misspell. Overshare.

Tell someone you miss them
even if they don't say it back.
Laugh like a madman.
Ugly, loud, breathless.
Laughter that makes strangers turn.
Laughter that doesn't apologize.

Let your nose turn red,
your eyes water,
Your mascara bleeds like art.

Save that child.
The one inside you,
the one who loved too much,
the one who never got picked,
the one who feared the dark and still does.

Protect her from the world's cynicism.
From growing too serious,
too normal,
too numb.

Learn to write without fear,
to dance when no one claps,
to cry when needed
and laugh without a reason.

Believe—
in kindness,
in madness,
in miracles.

Let her fall in love with her chaos.
Let her be the kind of woman
who howls at the moon
and still reads bedtime stories to herself.

Because this life,
this strange, brief, breathtaking life—
was never meant to be lived in straight lines.
So, eat the fog.
Break the script.
Save the child.
Write the revolution
with bare feet and burning heart.

14. "The Eyes, Chico"

Genuinity lies in the eyes of the beholder—
in the way they soften at beauty,
pause at pain,
and flicker in moments of raw truth.

It exists in our innocence.
It lingers in the pauses between words.
It stays—quietly. Forever.

And it's strange
how easy it is to recognize genuine people—
as if our souls have secret antennas.

They find ways to stay true
amidst the cold,
the condensed,
the morphed bodies passing by.

An honest man carries his entire life in his eyes.
Every heartbreak. Every hope.
Every unfinished dream.

You'll spot him in a crowd—
not by volume,
but by the way, silence settles around him,
like trust in its purest form.

He doesn't need to be understood,
just witnessed.
Because some souls speak in stillness,
and some truths are too sacred for sound.

He might be destroyed,
devastated,
demanding,
or dreamy—

But he will always be there.
Right there.
Because the eyes, Chico—
They never LIE.

15. "Those Melancholic Eyes"

There's a sadness tucked in all our eyes—
silent, ancient, never asking why.
We run from it in hurried strides,
into arms, into work, into stories we hide.

We make love, bake pies,
and binge-watch tales to hush our cries.
We listen to laughter, strangers, and lore,
hoping to drown that ache in our core.

But the eyes, oh, those eyes,
carry the weight of unspoken skies.
They hold desire, grief, a desperate plea
for touch, truth, and for someone to see.

They echo agony and gasp for grace,
searching for comfort in a lover's embrace.
They crave to be heard, to be whole, to be held,
to silence the chaos we've secretly felt.

We sprint toward food, toward noise and the crowd,
toward work and to love that screams out loud.
To mothers, to memories, to stories and men,
running from something we'll feel again.

It has nothing to do with the life we portray—
not the praise, the job, or the roles we play.
It stays like a ghost in the back of our mind,
whispering truths we never define.

And the tragedy? We know.
We know it well.
But we don't speak. We don't tell.
We are terrified—
of our melancholic spell.

We plan and pretend,
"Someday, it'll end."
Once we're in love, once we belong,
once we write that perfect lifelong song—
with a pup, a home, a garden in spring,
Surely then the eyes will lose their sting.

But they return.
On pizza nights,
in paused episodes of borrowed lives,

in silence that speaks more than sound—
They crawl back in, unannounced.

You feel it.
The longing.
The thirst.
The hollow bloom of hunger cursed.

And so, what now?
We accept the blue.
We let it stay,
like an old friend too true.

And if you ask me what I do
when those eyes demand their due—
I write.
Of course I do.

Pen bleeding thoughts I dare not say.
That's my rebellion.
My romance.
My way.

16. "Romanticing Time: The Ultimate Revolution"

All I want to convey is
It won't take long.
You can spare me a cheese sandwich
Or a song.
The dynamics of this universe's manifestation
of my motion can be transverse or perpendicular.
All you truly see is the dynamism of space.
I'm here in this moment,
and I ran out on your face.
I'm the reason you'll see tomorrow.
Does it exist? I don't care.
Just like your grief, your borrowed sorrow.
You tap my shoulder, ask me to stop.
See?
I slowed down for the depth of your talk.
You think I'm too little or too heavy to carry.
But I live in your mind,
frosted with cream and cherries.
Species like yours try to test me

calculate, define, draw a graph,
Write a theory.
But little do you know,
I change
for every fate and face.
Nowhere to be found,
yet I exist in every place.
Worship me as a god,
or call me a secret,
my mate;
I'm you.
I'm everybody.
I'm Newton.
I'm Faraday.
I'm the massive neutron star.
I'm the flower you clicked
the mountain you love
from afar.
Do you need me today?
I won't bother
to drop a hi.
But when you beg me
to pass in seconds
I'll sit beside you
with a long
cup of chai.
They say I'm found

in Special Theory of Relativity.
Yes, I've heard of the guy
who studied me thoroughly.
I am the "forever" you crave
in love's dimension.
I am the sixteen directions
your beyond, your ascension.
So, all I came to say is:
It won't take long.
You keep changing your space
but you'll find
I've been with you
all along.

17. "In the End, We Begin"

We die;
We all do.
But energies live,
and names survive.
Our experiments echo—
proof that our contributions weren't futile.
We die;
We all do.
Yet love lives.
Memories fill the void.
Our children breathe the same gaseous molecules—
the oxygen we once survived.
We die;
We all do.
But our frequencies remain.
The old glasses we wore,
the belief systems we clung to,
our rituals and routines,
like fingerprints in dust.

We die;

We all do.

But stories live.

The love gossips you once shared.

The grandma's ghost tales and her stitched-up values,

woven quietly into family seams.

We die;

We all do.

But maybe we don't.

Maybe we shift.

Maybe we survive in some undiscovered dimension,

waiting to be known.

We die;

We all do.

Let's believe that—

for now.

Or maybe it's *you*, calling you.

Hey, a book just dropped into your room.

We die;

We all do.

But is the body in the mind—

or the mind in the body?

Are souls just switching skins,

or simply pure energies,

wandering unmeasured?

We die.
We all do.
But perhaps in dreams,
we visit our former selves—
whispering wisdom through déjà vu.
Perhaps the wind knows our name,
and trees remember our touch.
Perhaps every sunset
is a life folding into light just to rise again.
We die;
We all do.
And yet
forever remains,
and nothing does, too.
Our presence is felt nowhere.
Or maybe we live
Everywhere.
We die.
We all do.

18. "Does the revolution ever die?"

I shut my eyelids—
and the revolution drops dead.
The world clutters itself
with the death of the insignificant,
parading beauty and chaos alike,
bringing the best and the worst
to pound at my chest
and ache through my bones.

But my head hums
the mutiny song of my heart—
a soft, steady anthem
of peaceful uprisings
and favorite war songs.
the lullabies I whisper
just to fall asleep.

I was born for this revolution.
I didn't ask for it—
and yet, I always ask:

What is this delirious resolve?
Why did I ever want to rebel?

I bleed in metaphors
because reality cuts too deep.
My breath, a whispered manifesto—
my existence, quiet defiance.

But the answer sings back—
Renaissance flows in my arteries,
killing the tumor of stagnation,
igniting my blood with questions
I'm too exhausted to answer.

What is it?
What am I here for—
Imprisonment or salvation?

19. "IF"

If you can do everything and still not lose your self-
esteem,
If you can listen to all and yet not become anyone's
shadow,
If you can respect every faith while holding on to your
own,
If you can welcome failure and choose to amend, do not
retreat.

If you can see the world in shades of grey,
and still not let go of your core values,
If you can recognize faces behind masks,
yet smile with sincerity anyway,

If you can know the duality of your work,
yet walk steadily with purpose in your stride,
If you can win the world
but still risk it all in one honest gamble.

If you can reach the top
and not curse the silence of altitude,
If you can be firm in your resolve
and still bend when the wind demands it,

If you can know the flaws in others
and still love them as they are.
If you can know nothing truly matters—
and still sweat, strive, still build.

If you can lend an ear to everyone
but act only when your soul calls out,
If you can walk with the crowd
and still honor every varied step.

If you can love deeply, truly—
without the cost of your self-respect.
If you can stay alive and still acknowledge
that death waits for all alike.

If you can touch the sky
and still know—it's only an illusion,
Then—
Yours is the Earth and the sky,
and above all,
You are a HUMAN, My friend.

20. "The Storm Is You"

Sometimes,
fate whirls like a sandstorm—
small, shifting,
turning on the heels of your every escape.
You pivot.
It follows.
You retreat.
It adjusts.
An ominous dance with death before dawn,
and you ask—why?
Because this storm,
this furious swirl of dust and bone,
was never born beyond the horizon.
It lives within you.
You are the storm.
And so you step in.
Eyes shut.
Ears closed.
No sun, no moon, no axis of time.

Just fine white dust
like the powdered bones of forgotten selves,
rising, writhing.
You walk,
even as it carves your flesh—
a thousand blades
of memory, grief, rage.
You bleed.
You hold the blood—
yours, and theirs.
And when the storm passes—if it does—
you won't recall how you survived.
You won't even be sure if it is over.
But one thing—
one sacred, brutal truth will remain.

You are not
the same soul
who stepped into the wind.

THAT'S WHAT THE STORM WAS ALWAYS FOR!